A FOOTPRINT ON THE AIR

A FOOTPRINT ON THE AIR

an anthology of nature verse

Selected by Naomi Lewis

Illustrated by Liz Graham-Yooll

Hutchinson

London Melbourne Sydney Auckland Johannesburg

Hutchinson Junior Books Ltd
An imprint of the Hutchinson Publishing Group
17–21 Conway Street, London W1P 6JD
Hutchinson Group (Australia) Pty Ltd
30–32 Cremorne Street, Richmond South, Victoria 3121
PO Box 151, Broadway, New South Wales 2007
Hutchinson Group (NZ) Ltd
32–34 View Road, PO Box 40086, Glenfield, Auckland 10
Hutchinson Group (SA) (Pty) Ltd
PO Box 337, Bergvlei 2012, South Africa
First published 1983

Set in Baskerville by Bookens, Saffron Walden, Essex

Printed in Great Britain by The Anchor Press Ltd
and bound by Wm Brendon & Son Ltd, both of Tiptree, Essex

British Library Cataloguing in Publication Data
Lewis, Naomi
    A footprint on the air.
    1. Children's poetry, English   2. Nature—
Juvenile poetry
    I. Title   II. Graham-Yooll, Elizabeth
    821'.008'036   PZ8.3
        ISBN 0 09 152720 1

Contents

Introduction 8

A Footprint on the Air *Naomi Lewis* 13

I HAVE A FAWN

I Have a Fawn *Thomas Moore* (extract) 15

Ha, Snow *T. E. Brown* (extract) 16

Hedgehog *Leonard Clark* 17

Hare *Adele Davide* 18

White Hare *Anna Wickham* 18

Anne and the Fieldmouse *Ian Serraillier* 19

The Goat Paths *James Stephens* 20

Out in the Dark *Edward Thomas* 24

Of Jeoffry, His Cat *Christopher Smart* (extract) 26

The Tenant *Ursula Stuart Laird* 28

The Hound of Ulster *Stevie Smith* 29

A Fox Met in a Dream *John May* 30

A Night with a Wolf *Bayard Taylor* 32

Stopping by Woods on a Snowy Evening
Robert Frost 34

A Small Dragon *Brian Patten* 35

Two Songs of a Fool *W. B. Yeats* 36

Family Holiday *Raymond Wilson* 38

My Mother Saw a Dancing Bear *Charles Causley* 39

JENNY WREN AND ROBIN

Jenny Wren and Robin *Anon*   40

The Budgie *Stanley Cook*   41

Three Turkeys *Marjory Fleming* (aged 7)   42

The Aziola *Percy Bysshe Shelley*   43

Storm *Walter de la Mare*   44

Yellow Bird *Arthur Waley*   45

Yesterday I Heard a Thrush *Harold Monro*   46

Hoo, Hoo, Hoo *Anon*   46

Pigeon *Naomi Lewis*   47

THE FLOWER AND THE LEAF

Ferns *Gene Baro*   48

Henry and Mary *Robert Graves*   49

What is Pink? *Christina Rossetti*   50

Growing Grass *Stanley Cook*   51

The Nightingale *Ian Colvin*   52

The Song of Blodeuwedd *Anon*   53

The Two Roots *Christian Morgenstern*   54

It Rains *Edward Thomas*   55

Summer Dawn *William Morris*   56

The Woodspurge *Dante Gabriel Rossetti*   57

Mushrooms *Sylvia Plath*   58

THEY CREEP THEY CRAWL THEY HOP THEY SWIM

An Anglo-Saxon Riddle   60

The Butterfly in Church   *William Cowper*   61

The Herring   *Anon*   61

Clock-a-Clay   *John Clare*   62

Silverfish, Spiders and Flies   *Stanley Cook*   63

The Worm   *Raymond Souster*   64

Considering the Snail   *Thom Gunn*   65

A Narrow Fellow in the Grass   *Emily Dickinson*   66

First Song   *Galway Kinnell*   68

Julius Caesar and the Honey Bee
  Charles Tennyson Turner   69

Legend   *Kay Hargreaves*   70

Goldfish   *Alan Jackson*   71

END PIECE

Happiness   *Erica Marx*   72

Acknowledgements   75

Introduction

What *is* a genuine animal poem? One, I would say, that presents an animal as itself, with its own gifts and qualities. Though in the poem we *see* the bird or beast from the human view, the same poem also attempts to catch for a moment the spirit of the creature. You may find this, say, in Edward Thomas's deer, part of the night; in James Stephen's marvellous light-foot goats, like airy thoughts; in Shelley's haunting aziola, in John May's fox, so reasonably asking for its share. Marjory Fleming, at seven, prefers to take a farmyard death from the turkey's view. The only poem I have ever met about a silverfish is in this book.

Even between humans, who have the same speech, there is a final ghostly barrier. Between ourselves and animals, the captives, the toilers, even our closest pets, there is an invisible bridge which we cannot find to cross. (It is on the death of a cat or dog or horse that we may have known for years that this truth comes through. The language used has always been human language; we have never really known theirs.) This is the bridge that poems can sometimes leap over.

Yet books of so-called animal tales and verse are too often padded out with items that don't belong at all. Fables, the old traditional sort, are an example. *Fables?* Yes! It is high time to give a rest to all but a few of those mean little tales unjustly laying on animals the human vices of greed, vanity, falseness, cowardice and the rest. They are not animal attributes. (*King Log and King Stork* is one of the few that I'd keep.)

No less out of place in an honest book of animal verse is a certain kind of 'funny' rhyme, making a joke or comic turn of elephant, hippo, rhino, crocodile, camel, monkey, horse or ass. Yet these are serious creatures whose lives, through human abuse, are nearer to tragedy than to comedy. Animals simply are not (unintentionally) funny. They are nothing at all like the crude grotesques in the Disney-type cartoon pictures. I wonder how many of us have really seen a living, uncaged wolf, or fox (or even lamb) at no more than a hand's distance away. Yet the first thing we realize when we have this experience (through television or photographs if not in life) is that animals are essentially serious – not in a glum, self-pitying way, but because they need to be alert to every sound and movement in their world. With all animals, the nearer we approach the greater is their mystery – something never found in comic fables, pictures, cartoons and the like. The television camera is one way of bringing us close to this magic. Poetry can be another, and no less real or exact.

But what of the handful of oddities in this book, the nursery rhymes, magic and nonsense verses? And that frog, too, out of fairy tale? A good question – and an answer is to hand. In no case here is an animal unfairly burdened with human sins. The fairy tale frog is a respected character; as the rhyme goes:

Maidens, treat all frogs with care.
One may be the king's heir!

As for the nursery rhymes, to very young children animals are but another kind of human (nearer in size, less baffling possibly) as humans are but another kind of animal. All, to a child, have ranging powers and abilities that are not to be questioned in its new peculiar world. And Christian Morgenstern (1871-1914)? Like Edward Lear, his most notable predecessor in the field of nonsense he took the animal world most seriously. Young children will understand his squirrels perfectly well. A word that needs a searching look – you will find it often enough – is anthropomorphism, which means, more or less, attributing human qualities to non-human creatures and things (a car, a boat, the wind, a nation). It tends to be used as a term of scorn by people who don't want to think that animals feel pain, fear, boredom, grief or stress. Yet the same humans speak of a 'lazy', 'vicious' or 'spiteful' animal when they really mean a terrified, overworked or tormented one. Notice how, in big-game hunting, the victim is always called 'the brute':

Cet animal est méchant!
Quand on l'attaque, il se defend!

That's not hard to translate. Chesterton's ugly poem 'The Donkey'

9

is, I would say, a badly anthropomorphic poem. You can probably think of others. You will not find them in this book.

False myth (in verse or prose) isn't a harmless matter. It has almost caused the total genocide of the wolf, the most misjudged of all animals, and in ways too dreadful to set out here. Remember too that while every few days a *million* more humans are added to the earth, and another million before the week is out, every hour, as more and more of the green earth goes, the number of free great animals dwindles nearer to nought. Today the writer who turns to the animals' world, whether writing for children or adults, in prose or verse, has a major subject that is still largely unexplored. As for the wild flowers on Titania's bank or in Lycidas or in the old Welsh poem in this book, in life they might be classed as weeds, burned out with herbicides. How lucky that they survive in poetry.

Everyone who makes an anthology knows very well which poems remain outside. This may be too long, that may be so well known that another has been given a chance. One of the greatest animal poems ever written is Blake's 'Tyger' but that's easy to find elsewhere. A few poems here by contrast are published for the first time. Among those outside the door (so to speak) are several by D. H. Lawrence – 'Snake' and 'Tortoise' and 'Bat' and others; and several by Stevie Smith, not only those on cats (better than T. S. Eliot's, some consider) but her unforgettable 'The Best Beast of the Fat-stock Show, Earls Court'. Another of her marvellous poems is, happily, in the book. Read Hardy for his rare understanding of animals and birds; and Edward Thomas for the wild flowers, leaves and plants that grew into his own story, and practically everything ever written by John Clare, who knew the grasses, hedgerows, flowers, the insects and small animals better than any poet of his quality in the language.

Finally, here is a tale, a true one, which brings together, most strangely, the animal and the flower. In 1900, in a remote part of eastern Russia, a mammoth, which had lain for many thousands of years in the frozen earth, was seen near to the surface. When the news reached St Petersburg, three learned men, experts in

10

different fields, set out on the long hard journey east. They found the creature, still uncorrupt and clean – though of the humans who killed and probably ate its kind, no trace remained. Inside was its final supper – heather, mosses, grasses, flowers and seeds. Some of these seeds were planted and they grew.

That is a poem in itself.

Naomi Lewis

A Footprint on the Air

'Stay!' said the child. The bird said, 'No,
My wing has mended, I must go.
I shall come back to see you though,
One night, one day –'
                              'How shall I know?'
'Look for my footprint in the snow.'

'The snow soon goes – oh, that's not fair!'
'Don't grieve. Don't grieve. I shall be there
In the bright season of the year,
One night, one day –'
                              'But tell me, where?'
'Look for my footprint on the air.'

NAOMI LEWIS

I HAVE A FAWN

I Have a Fawn

I have a fawn from Aden's land,
On leafy buds and berries nursed;
And you shall feed him from your hand,
Though he may start with fear at first.
And I will lead you where he lies
For shelter in the noon-day heat:
And you may touch his sleeping eyes,
And feel his little silver feet.

THOMAS MOORE   (EXTRACT)

Ha, Snow

Ha, snow
Upon the crags!
How slow
The winter lags!
Ha, little lamb upon the crags,
How fearlessly you go!
Take care
Up there,
You little woolly atom! On and on
He goes . . . 'tis steep . . . Hillo,
My friend is gone!

T. E. BROWN (EXTRACT)

Hedgehog

Comes out by day in autumn,
exploring hedgehog, betrays himself
snoring loudly in leafy ditch;
plump with summer's fat, moves along,
battering slow way through dry twigs.
I hear him lumbering, hairy head appears,
then all his ten-inch prickly length,
makes for the bank, senses me there,
rolls into a ball, waits for the attack.
I leave him alone though, curled up on the hill's lip,
this earth-brown savage, enemy of frogs.
He'll chew beetles and mice to powder, hear
every small noise in undergrowth,
will take on snakes by the tail,
bayonet them with needle-spines.
Shy of the sun, dislikes company,
cannot see far, a fine swimmer,
drinks milk.

LEONARD CLARK

Hare

Midsummer madness
And the March hare
Galloping across fields
With nowhere to go but home
And happy for it.

ADELE DAVIDE

White Hare

Love, love, the dogs are after me,
I am transmuted to a White Hare.
You sit in the lighted house and
    cannot see,
I know that you are there.
See where I pass, a shadow on
    the grass,
Come swiftly,
Lift me to your care.

ANNA WICKHAM

Anne and the Fieldmouse

We found a mouse in the chalk quarry today
In a circle of stones and empty oil drums
By the fag end of a fire. There had been
A picnic there: he must have been after the crumbs.

Jane saw him first, a flicker of brown fur
In and out of the charred wood and chalk-white.
I saw him last, but not till we'd turned up
Every stone and surprised him into flight,

Though not far – little zigzags spurts from stone
To stone. Once, as he lurked in his hiding-place,
I saw his beady eyes uplifted to mine.
I'd never seen such terror in so small a face.

I watched, amazed and guilty. Beside us suddenly
A heavy pheasant whirred up from the ground,
Scaring us all; and, before we knew it, the mouse
Had broken cover, skimming away without a sound,

Melting into the nettles. We didn't go
Till I'd chalked in capitals on a rusty can:
THERE'S A MOUSE IN THOSE NETTLES. LEAVE
HIM ALONE. NOVEMBER 15TH ANNE.

IAN SERRAILLIER

The Goat Paths

The crooked paths
Go every way
Upon the hill
– They wind about
Through the heather,
In and out
Of a quiet
Sunniness.

And the goats,
Day after day,
Stray
In sunny
Quietness;
Cropping here
And cropping there
– As they pause,
And turn,
And pass
Now a bit
Of heather spray,
Now a mouthful
Of the grass.

In the deeper
Sunniness;
In the place
Where nothing stirs;
Quietly
In quietness:
In the quiet
Of the furze
They stand a while;
If you approach
They dream;
They run away!
They lie;
They will stare,
They stare
And stamp,
Upon the roving sky.
And bound,
With a sudden angry sound,
To the sunny
Quietude;
To crouch again,
Where nothing stirs,
In the quiet
Of the furze:
To crouch them down again,
And brood,
In the sunny
Solitude.

Were I but
As free
As they,
I would stray
Away
And brood;
I would beat
A hidden way,
Through the quiet
Heather spray,
To a sunny
Solitude.
And should you come
I'd run away!
I would make an angry sound,
I would stare,
And stamp,
And bound
To the deeper
Quietude;
To the place
Where nothing stirs
In the quiet
Of the furze.

In that airy
  Quietness
    I would dream
      As long as they:
        Through the quiet
          Sunniness
            I would stray
              Away
                And brood,
                  All among
                    The heather spray,
                      In a sunny
                        Solitude.
 – I would think
    Until I found
      Something
        I can never find;
          – Something
            Lying
              On the ground
                In the bottom
                  Of my mind.

JAMES STEPHENS

Out in the Dark

Out in the dark over the snow
The fallow fawns invisible go
With the fallow doe;
And the winds blow
Fast as the stars are slow.

Stealthily the dark haunts round
And, when the lamp goes, without sound
At a swifter bound
Than the swiftest hound
Arrives, and all else is drowned;

And star and I and wind and deer,
Are in the dark together, – near,
Yet far, – and fear
Drums on my ear
In that sage company drear.

How weak and little is the light,
All the universe of sight,
Love and delight,
Before the might,
If you love it not, of night.

EDWARD THOMAS

25

Of Jeoffry, His Cat

For I will consider my Cat Jeoffry.

For he is the servant of the Living God, duly and
daily serving him.

For this is done by wreathing his body seven times
round with elegant quickness.

For having done duty and received blessings he
begins to consider himself

For first he looks upon his fore-paws to see if
they are clean.

For secondly he kicks up behind to clear away there.

For thirdly he works it upon stretch with the fore-
paws extended.

For fourthly he sharpens his paws by wood.

For fifthly he washes himself.

For sixthly he rolls upon wash.

For seventhly he fleas himself, that he may not be
interrupted upon the beat.

For eighthly he rubs himself against a post.

For ninthly he looks up for his instructions.

For tenthly he goes in quest of food.

For having consider'd God and himself he will
   consider his neighbour.
For if he meets another cat he will kiss her in
   kindness.
For when he takes his prey he plays with it to give
   it a chance.
For when his day's work is done his business more
   properly begins.
For he keeps the Lord's watch in the night against
   the adversary.
For he counteracts the powers of darkness by his
   electrical skin and glaring eyes.
For he counteracts the Devil, who is death, by
   brisking about the life.
For he purrs in thankfulness, when God tells him
   he's a good Cat.
For every house is incomplete without him and a
   blessing is lacking in the spirit.

CHRISTOPHER SMART (EXTRACT)

The Tenant

Five people live in the house
untidily, inconsistently:
The proper tenant
is Lucky Baby
the kitten who
came like a squatter,
but now has her
territory clearly marked,
who knows meals
should be on time
and eaten delicately,
without hurrying;
fresh water available,
and a place to keep
the draught away.
She knows her inherited rights
without having to
form a committee,
or elect an MP.

URSULA STUART LAIRD

The Hound of Ulster

Little boy
Will you stop
And take a look
In the puppy shop –
Dogs blue and liver
Noses aquiver
Little dogs big dogs
Dogs for sport and pleasure
Fat dogs meagre dogs
Dogs for lap and leisure.
Do you see that wire-haired terrier?
Could anything be merrier?
Do you see that Labrador retriever?
His name is Belvoir*.
Thank you courteous stranger, said the child,
    By your words I am beguiled,
    But tell me I pray
    What lurks in the gray
    Cold shadows at the back of the shop?
Little boy do not stop
Come away
From the puppy shop.
For the Hound of Ulster lies tethered there
Cuchulain tethered by his golden hair
His eyes are closed and his lips are pale
Hurry little boy he is not for sale.

STEVIE SMITH

*PRONOUNCED LIKE BEAVER

A Fox Met in a Dream

There came to me a fox
So hard put to catch his natural prey
That he asked me quite openly,
And with that underlying truth
That comes from being driven by life's conditions,
If he might steal from me one fowl.

At first I thought to dispatch his very life
For being so impudent.
But then I woke
And called my hounds to heel
And permitted him to go about his want.

The fox
Bearing his gift,
Which I had so mistakenly thought was mine to give
And not his by equal right,
Started up the hill
To feed his young.

But alas, at this point,
Owing to the preceding emotion of beneficence,
I fell asleep – jumped up, and from the concealment
  of a tree,
Shot him from afar off.

Poor beast.
He never heard the shot that killed him.
But alas
The distance was not quite far enough to drown
His long sad cry
That woke me from my sleep.

JOHN MAY

A Night with a Wolf

High up on the lonely mountains,
    Where the wild men watched and waited;
Wolves in the forest, and bears in the bush,
    And I on my path belated.

The rain and the night together
    Came down, and the wind came after,
Bending the props of the pine-tree roof,
    And snapping many a rafter.

I crept along in the darkness,
    Stunned, and bruised, and blinded;
Crept to a fir with thick-set boughs,
    And a sheltering rock behind it.

There, from the blowing and raining,
    Crouching, I sought to hide me.
Something rustled; two green eyes shone;
    And a wolf lay down beside me!

His wet fur pressed against me;
    Each of us warmed the other;
Each of us felt, in the stormy dark,
    That beast and man were brother.

And when the falling forest
    No longer crashed in warning,
Each of us went from our hiding place
    Forth in the wild, wet morning.

BAYARD TAYLOR

Stopping by Woods
on a Snowy Evening

Whose woods these are I think I know.
His house is in the village though;
He will not see me stopping here
To watch his woods fill up with snow.

My little horse must think it queer
To stop without a farmhouse near
Between the woods and frozen lake
The darkest evening of the year.

He gives his harness bells a shake
To ask if there is some mistake.
The only other sound's the sweep
Of easy wind and downy flake.

The woods are lovely, dark and deep,
But I have promises to keep,
And miles to go before I sleep,
And miles to go before I sleep.

ROBERT FROST

A Small Dragon

I've found a small dragon in the woodshed.
Think it must have come from deep inside a forest
because its damp and green and leaves
are still reflecting in its eyes.

I fed it on many things, tried grass,
the roots of stars, hazel-nut and dandelion,
but it stared up at me as if to say, I need
foods you can't provide.

It made a nest among the coal,
not unlike a bird's but larger,
it is out of place here
and is quite silent.

If you believed in it I would come
hurrying to your house to let you share my wonder,
but I want instead to see
if you yourself will pass this way.

BRIAN PATTEN

Two Songs of a Fool

I

A speckled cat and a tame hare
Eat at my hearthstone
And sleep there;
And both look up to me alone
For learning and defence
As I look up to Providence.

I start out of my sleep to think
Some day I may forget
Their food and drink;
Or, the house door left unshut,
The hare may run till it's found
The horn's sweet note and the tooth of the hound.

I bear a burden that might well try
Men that do all by rule,
And what can I
That am a wandering-witted fool
But pray to God that He ease
My great responsibilities?

II

I slept on my three-legged stool by the fire;
The speckled cat slept on my knee;
We never thought to enquire
Where the brown hare might be,
And whether the door were shut.
Who knows how she drank the wind
Stretched up on two legs from the mat,
Before she had settled her mind
To drum with her heel and to leap?
Had I but awakened from sleep
And called her name, she had heard,
It may be, and had not stirred,
That now, it may be, has found
The horn's sweet note and the tooth of the hound.

W. B. YEATS

Family Holiday

Eight months ago, on Christmas Day,
he was a present for the twins,
a toy to join in all their play.

They left by car, but how long since
he cannot tell, nor when they'll come
(if ever) back, to make amends.

The house is blind and deaf and dumb,
the curtains drawn, the windows shut,
the doors sealed tighter than a tomb.

Even the little garden hut
is padlocked. He barks feebly at
each slowing car or passing foot.

Stretched on the WELCOME on the mat
in the front porch, he feels the hunger
gnawing inside him like a rat.

Suffers, endures, but knows no anger.

RAYMOND WILSON

My Mother Saw a Dancing Bear

My mother saw a dancing bear
By the schoolyard, a day in June.
The keeper stood with chain and bar
And whistle-pipe, and played a tune.

And Bruin lifted up its head
And lifted up its dusty feet,
And all the children laughed to see
It caper in the summer heat.

They watched as for the Queen it died.
They watched it march. They watched it halt.
They heard the keeper as he cried,
'Now, roly-poly! Somersault!'

And then, my mother said, there came
the keeper with a begging-cup,
The bear with burning coat of fur,
Shaming the laughter to a stop.

They paid a penny for the dance,
But what they saw was not the show;
Only, in Bruin's aching eyes,
Far-distant forests, and the snow.

CHARLES CAUSLEY

JENNY WREN AND ROBIN

Jenny Wren and Robin

Jenny Wren fell sick
   Upon a merry time,
in came Robin Redbreast
   And brought her sops and wine.

Eat well of the sop, Jenny,
   Drink well of the wine.
Thank you, Robin, kindly,
   You shall be mine.

Jenny Wren got well,
   And stood upon her feet;
And told Robin plainly,
   She loved him not a bit.

Robin he got angry,
   And hopped upon a twig,
Saying, out upon you, fie upon you!
   Bold faced jig!

NURSERY RHYME

The Budgie

The budgie has a bell to ring
And tunes from the radio to sing
A pot of water and pot of seed
For when he wants to drink or feed.
And every week a new sandsheet
To sharpen the claws of his bony feet.
He calls himself a pretty boy
But his only friend is a plastic toy.

Yet budgies fly in another land
Over miles of yellow sand
And peck the seeds that grow
And drink the streams that flow.
A crowd of uncaged budgies fly,
Green as grass or blue as sky.

STANLEY COOK

41

Three Turkeys

Three Turkeys fair their last have breathed
And now this worled for ever leaved.
Their Father & their Mother too
Will sigh and weep as well as you,
Mourning for their osprings[1] fair
whom they did nurse with tender care.
Indeed the rats their bones have cranched
To eternity they are launched.
Their graceful form and pretty eyes
Their fellow fows[2] did not despise,
A direful death indeed they had
That would put any parent mad,
But she was more than usual calm
She did not give a singel dam
She is as gentel as a lamb,
Here ends this melancholy lay
Farewell Poor Turkeys I must say.

MARJORY FLEMING (AGED 7)

[1]offspring
[2]fowls
Marjory Fleming's original spelling has been retained

MARJORY FLEMING (1803–11) WAS SEVEN WHEN SHE WROTE
THIS FORTHRIGHT POEM: A YEAR AND A HALF LATER SHE
WAS DEAD. SHE COULD NOT HAVE GUESSED AT HER LATER
FAME, FOR VANITY IN HER NATIVE EDINBURGH WAS NOT
ENCOURAGED.

The Aziola

I

'Do you not hear the Aziola cry?
  Methinks she must be nigh,'
 Said Mary, as we sate
In dusk, ere stars were lit, or candles brought;
  And I, who thought
This Aziola was some tedious woman,
  Asked, 'Who is Aziola?' How elate
I felt to know that it was nothing human,
  No mockery to myself to fear or hate:
  And Mary saw my soul,
And laughed, and said, 'Disquiet yourself not;
  'Tis nothing but a little downy owl.'

II

Sad Aziola! many an eventide
  Thy music I had heard
By wood and stream, meadow and mountain-side,
  And fields and marshes wide, –
Such as nor voice, nor lute, nor wind, nor bird,
  The soul ever stirred;
Unlike and far sweeter than them all.
Sad Aziola! from that moment I
  Loved thee and thy sad cry.

PERCY BYSSHE SHELLEY

Storm

First there were two of us, then there were three of
    us,
Then there was one bird more,
Four of us – wild white sea-birds,
Treading the ocean floor;
And the wind rose, and the sea rose,
To the angry billow's roar –
With one of us – two of us – three of us – four of us
Sea-birds on the shore.

Soon there were five of us, soon there were nine of
    us,
And lo! in a trice sixteen!
And the yeasty surf curdled over the sands,
The gaunt grey rocks between;
And the tempest raved, and the lightning's fire
Struck blue on the spindrift hoar –
And on four of us – ay, and on four times four of us
Sea-birds on the shore.

And our sixteen waxed to thirty-two,
And they to past three score –
A wild, white welter of winnowing wings,
And ever more and more,
And the winds lulled, and the sea went down,
And the sun streamed out on high,
Gilding the pools and the spume and the spars
'Neath the vast blue deeps of the sky;

And the isles and the bright green headlands shone,
As they'd never shone before,
Mountains and valleys of silver cloud,
Wherein to swing, sweep, soar –
A host of screeching, scolding, scrabbling
Sea-birds on the shore –
A snowy, silent, sun-washed drift
Of sea-birds on the shore.

WALTER DE LA MARE

Yellow Bird

In the high trees – many doleful winds:
The ocean waters – dashed into waves.
If the sharp sword be not in your hand,
How can you hope your friends will remain many?

Do you not see that sparrow on the fence?
Seeing the hawk it casts itself into the snare:
The Young Man to see the sparrow grieves;
He takes his sword and cuts through the netting.
The yellow sparrow flies away, away,
away, away, up to the blue sky
And down again to thank the young Man.

WU-TI, EMP. OF LIANG DYNASTY (AD 464–549)

ARTHUR WALEY FROM THE ORIGINAL CHINESE

Yesterday I Heard a Thrush

Yesterday I heard a thrush;
He held me with his eyes:
I waited on my yard of earth,
He watched me from his skies.

My whole day was penetrated
By his wild and windy cries,
And the glitter of his eyes.

HAROLD MONRO

Hoo, Hoo, Hoo

Once I was a monarch's daughter,
And sat on a lady's knee:
But now I am a nightly rover
Banished to the ivy tree.

Crying hoo, hoo, hoo, hoo, hoo,
Hoo, hoo, hoo, my feet are cold.

Pity me, for here you see me
Persecuted, poor, and old.

ANON

Pigeon

A Haiku

Piccadilly light . . .
On the pavement pecks a bird,
Doesn't know it's night.

NAOMI LEWIS

THE FLOWER
AND THE LEAF

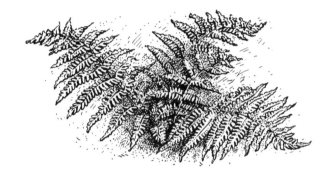

Ferns

High, high in the branches
the seawinds plunge and roar.
A storm is moving westward,
but here on the forest floor
the ferns have captured stillness.
A green sea growth they are.

The ferns lie underwater
in a light of the forest's green.
Their motion is like stillness,
as if water shifts between
and a great storm quivers
through fathoms of green.

GENE BARO

48

Henry and Mary

Henry was a young king,
  Mary was his queen;
He gave her a snowdrop
  On a stalk of green.

Then all for his kindness
  And all for his care
She gave him a new-laid egg
  In the garden there.

'Love, can you sing?'
               'I cannot sing.'
'Or tell a tale?'
             'Not one I know.'
'Then let us play at queen and king
  As down the garden walks we go.'

ROBERT GRAVES

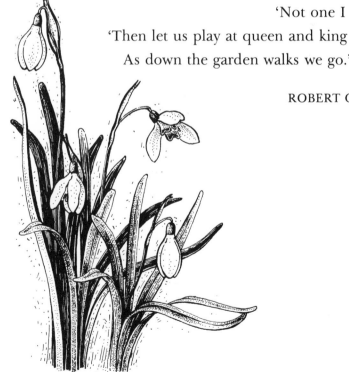

What is Pink?

What is pink? A rose is pink
By the fountain's brink.
What is red? A poppy's red
In its barley bed.
What is blue? The sky is blue
Where the clouds float through.
What is white? A swan is white
Sailing in the light.
What is yellow? Pears are yellow,
Rich and ripe and mellow.
What is green? The grass is green,
With small flowers between.
What is violet? Clouds are violet
In the summer twilight.
What is orange? Why, an orange,
Just an orange!

CHRISTINA ROSSETTI

Growing Grass

Grass grows anywhere
Making the ground soft to the feet
And sowing the dust the wind puffs
Into holes and cracks with its
                              yellow seed.

On tumbledown old houses
It climbs the roof to sit on top.
Grass instead of smoke
Gathers round the chimney pot.

So when we set its seed
In a trough of polystyrene
No wonder grass came up
As long as hair and beautifully green.

We planted flowers as well –
Daffodils and Busy Lizzie.
When the grass grew really long
We gave it a haircut with our scissors.

Farmers grow grass in fields
To feed their cows non-stop all week.
We grew grass in a trough
For our guinea pigs to eat.

STANLEY COOK

The Nightingale

On his little twig of plum,
　His plum-tree twig, the nightingale
Dreamed one night that snow had come,
　On the hill and in the vale,
　In the vale and on the hill,
　Everything soft and white and still,
Only the snowflakes falling, falling,
　Only the snow . . .

On a night when the snow had come,
　As the snowflakes fell, the nightingale
Dreamed of orchards white with plum,
　On the hill and in the vale,
　In the vale and on the hill,
　Everything soft and white and still,
Only the petals falling, falling,
　Only the plum . . .

IAN COLVIN

FROM A JAPANESE NURSERY RHYME

The Song of Blodeuwedd

Not of father nor of mother
Was my blood, was my body,
I was spellbound by Gwydion,
Prime enchanter of the Britons,
When he formed me from nine blossoms,
   Nine buds of various kind:
From primrose of the mountain,
Broom, meadow-sweet and cockle,
   Together intertwined,
From the bean in its shade bearing
A white spectral army
   Of earth, of earthy kind,
From blossoms of the nettle,
Oak, thorn and bashful chestnut –
Nine powers of nine flowers,
   Nine powers in me combined,
   Nine buds of plant and tree.
Long and white are my fingers
   As the ninth wave of the sea.

FROM THE MEDIEVAL WELSH

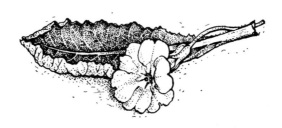

The Two Roots

A pair of pine roots, old and dark
make conversation in the park.

The whispers where the top leaves grow
are echoed in the roots below.

An aged squirrel sitting there
is knitting stockings for the pair.

The one says: squeak. The other: squawk.
That is enough for one day's talk.

CHRISTIAN MORGENSTERN

TRANSLATED BY MAX KNIGHT

It Rains

It rains, and nothing stirs within the fence
Anywhere through the orchard's untrodden, dense
Forest of parsley. The great diamonds
Of rain on the grassblades there is none to break,
Or the fallen petals further down to shake.

And I am nearly as happy as possible
To search the wilderness in vain though well,
To think of two walking, kissing there,
Drenched, yet forgetting the kisses of the rain:
Sad, too, to think that never, never again,

Unless alone, so happy shall I walk
In the rain. When I turn away, on its fine stalk
Twilight has fined to naught, the parsley flower
Figures, suspended still and ghostly white,
The past hovering as it revisits the light.

EDWARD THOMAS

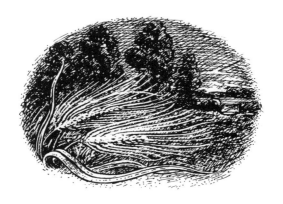

Summer Dawn

Pray but one prayer for me 'twixt thy closed lips;
   Think but one thought of me up in the stars.
The summer night waneth, the morning light slips,
   Faint and grey 'twixt the leaves of the aspen,
     betwixt the cloud bars,
That are patiently waiting there for the dawn:
   Patient and colourless, though Heaven's gold
Waits to float through them along with the sun.

Far out in the meadows, above the young corn,
   The heavy elms wait, and restless and cold
The uneasy wind rises; the roses are dun;
They pray the long gloom through, for daylight
   new born,
Round the lone house in the midst of the corn.
   Speak but one word to me over the corn,
     Over the tender, bow'd locks of the corn.

WILLIAM MORRIS

The Woodspurge

The wind flapped loose, the wind was still,
Shaken out dead from tree and hill:
I had walked on at the wind's will, –
I sat now, for the wind – as still.

Between my knees my forehead was, –
My lips, drawn in, said not Alas!
My hair was over in the grass,
My naked ears heard the day pass.

My eyes, wide open, had the run
Of some ten weeds to fix upon;
Among those few, out of the sun,
The woodspurge flowered, three cups in one.

From perfect grief there need not be
Wisdom or even memory:
One thing then learnt remains to me, –
The woodspurge has a cup of three.

DANTE GABRIEL ROSSETTI

Mushrooms

Overnight, very
Whitely, discreetly,
Very quietly
Our toes, our noses
Take hold of the loam,
Acquire the air.

Nobody sees us,
Stops us, betrays us;
The small grains make room.

Soft fists insist on
Heaving the needles,
The leafy bedding.

Even the paving;
Our hammers, our rams,
Earless and eyeless.

Perfectly voiceless,
Widen the crannies,
Shoulder through holes. We

Diet on water,
On crumbs of shadow,
Bland-mannered, asking

Little or nothing.
So many of us!
So many of us!

We are shelves, we are
Tables, we are meek,
We are edible,

Nudgers and shovers
In spite of ourselves.
Our kind multiplies;

We shall by morning
Inherit the earth.
Our foot's in the door

SYLVIA PLATH

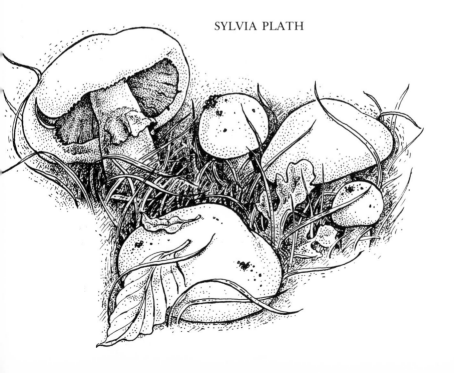

THEY CREEP
THEY CRAWL
THEY HOP
THEY SWIM

An Anglo-Saxon Riddle

A moth munched words. I thought that a marvel
(Told of these tidings), a tale of wonder
That a worm should swallow a man's wisdom,
A thief in darkness gnaw at his thinking,
The power of his song-stuff – and yet the stealer
Was no whit the wiser for the words eaten.

What am I?

TRANSLATED BY NAOMI LEWIS

WHEN THIS WAS WRITTEN WELL OVER A THOUSAND YEARS
AGO, POETRY DID NOT RHYME BUT HAD ITS OWN ECHOING
PATTERN OF REPEATED CONSONANTS, AS IN THIS VERSE.

ANSWER, AS YOU MAY HAVE GUESSED, IS A BOOKWORM. BOOK-
WORMS DO NOT SEEM SO FREQUENT TODAY – BUT THEN, LONG
AGO BOOKS WERE MADE OF TASTIER MATERIALS.

The Butterfly in Church

Butterfly, butterfly, why come you here?
  This is no bower for you;
Go, sip the honey-drop sweet and clear,
  Or bathe in the morning dew.

This is the place to think of heaven,
  This is the place to pray;
You have no sins to be forgiven –
  Butterfly, go away!

WILLIAM COWPER

The Herring

The herring loves the merry moonlight
And the mackerel loves the wind,
But the oyster loves the dredging song
For he comes of a gentle kind.

ANON

Clock-a-Clay

In the cowslip pips I lie,
Hidden from the buzzing fly,
While green grass beneath me lies,
Pearled with dew like fishes' eyes,
Here I lie, a clock-a-clay,
Waiting for the time of day.

While grassy forest quakes surprise,
And the wild wind sobs and sighs,
My gold home rocks as like to fall,
On its pillar green and tall;
When the pattering rain drives by
Clock-a-clay keeps warm and dry.

Day by day and night by night,
All the week I hide from sight;
In the cowslip pips I lie,
In rain and dew, still warm and dry;
Day and night and night and day,
Red, black-spotted clock-a-clay.

My home shakes in wind and showers,
Pale green pillar topped with flowers,
Bending at the wild wind's breath,
Till I touch the grass beneath;
Here I live, lone clock-a-clay,
Watching for the time of day.

JOHN CLARE   *Clock-a-Clay is a ladybird*

Silverfish, Spiders and Flies

Small creatures see
That none of the space
In our classroom
Goes to waste.

Silverfish keep warm
In cracks too small
Even for children's fingers
In the floor and against the wall.

And knitting their webs
The spiders fit
Onto ledges too narrow
For children to sit.

Flies stand on the ceiling
Or circle through the air
And even in P.E.
I never climbed up there.

Creatures that look
Like pips and seeds
Sow themselves in the places
No one else needs.

STANLEY COOK

The Worm

Don't ask me how he managed
to corkscrew his way
through the King Street Pavement,
I'll leave that to you.

All I know is
there he was,
circling, uncoiling
his shining three inches,
wiggling all ten toes
as the warm rain fell
in that dark morning street
of early April.

RAYMOND SOUSTER

Considering the Snail

The snail pushes through a green
night, for the grass is heavy
with water and meets over
the bright path he makes, where rain
has darkened the earth's dark. He
moves in a wood of desire,

pale antlers barely stirring
as he hunts. I cannot tell
what power is at work, drenched there
with purpose, knowing nothing.
What is a snail's fury? All
I think is that if later

I parted the blades above
the tunnel and saw the thin
trail of broken white across
litter, I would never have
imagined the slow passion
to that deliberate progress.

THOM GUNN

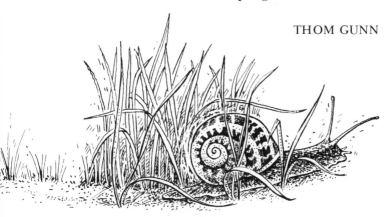

A Narrow Fellow in the Grass

A narrow fellow in the grass
Occasionally rides;
You may have met him – did you not?
His notice sudden is.

The grass divides as with a comb –
A spotted shaft is seen –
And then it closes at your feet
And opens further on.

He likes a boggy acre,
A floor too cool for corn –
Yet when a boy, and barefoot,
I more than once at morn

Have passed, I thought, a whip-lash
Unbraiding in the sun –
When, stooping to secure it,
It wrinkled, and was gone.

Several of nature's people
I know, and they know me –
I feel for them a transport
Of cordiality –

But never met this fellow,
Attended or alone,
Without a tighter breathing
And zero at the bone.

EMILY DICKINSON

First Song

Then it was dusk in Illinois, the small boy
After an afternoon of carting dung
Hung on the rail fence, a sapped thing
Weary to crying. Dark was growing tall
And he began to hear the pond frogs all
Calling upon his ear with what seemed their joy.

Soon their sound was pleasant for a boy
Listening in the smoky dusk and the nightfall
Of Illinois, and then from the field two small
Boys came bearing cornstalk violins
And rubbed three cornstalk bows with resins,
And they set fiddling with them as with joy.

It was now fine music, the frogs and the boys
Did in the towering Illinois twilight make
And into dark in spite of a right arm's ache
A boy's hunched body loved out of a stalk
The first song of his happiness, and the song woke
His heart to the darkness and into the sadness of joy.

GALWAY KINNELL

Julius Caesar and the Honey Bee

Poring on Caesar's death with earnest eye,
I heard a fretful buzzing in the pane:
'Poor bee!' I cried, 'I'll help thee by and by,'
Then dropp'd mine eyes upon the page again.
Alas! I did not rise; I help'd him not:
In the great voice of Roman history
I lost the pleading of the window bee,
And all his woes and troubles were forgot.
In pity for the mighty chief who bled
Beside his rival's statue, I delay'd
To serve the little insect's present need,
And so he died for lack of human aid.

I could not change the Roman's destiny:
I might have set the honey-maker free.

CHARLES TENNYSON TURNER

69

Legend

Down-dripping water led her
With its follow-me song
Away one morning
From the roses in the garden.
And she followed its call
Because she was bored with all
The roses.

Sliding slip-slop off the sloping leaves
Silver-lit and shimmering
She found at the end of it all
A great grey stone and frog.

Entranced by the moment,
Sure of enchantment,
She bent while it stayed still, still,
And kissed it.

Oh what a wailing and a-lack-a-day!
Oh what a tossing of grasses
What a beating of bushes
and ladies-in-waiting
Who waited in vain.

Under sloping-silver leaves,
Listening to the water-song,
Sat two frogs.

But no-one noticed them.

KAY HARGREAVES

Goldfish

the scene of the crime
was a goldfish bowl
goldfish were kept
in the bowl at the time:

that was the scene
and that was the crime

ALAN JACKSON

END PIECE

Happiness

When I, but hedge-high
And meadow-sweet tall
Rambled the countryside,
My nose,
Gay with the sweet smell
Of bramble and briar,
The rose of the hedgerows
        all mine,
And the powder of moth-wing and butterfly,
Motes in the lanes of the sun –
        All was well.
The fire of distant stars in the night
Was also my height,
And the rocket of rooks shot into the sky
Fell back on to earth, my playthings . . . I feel
O then there were skies to swim
And great seas to fly, and heaven was on the ground,
My paradise all found . . . .
And I did not need to kneel.

ERICA MARX

Acknowledgements

The compiler and publisher wish to thank the following for permission to use copyright material in this anthology:

Frederick Warne for 'Hedgehog' by Leonard Clark, from *Round about Nine* selected by Geoffrey Palmer and Noel Lloyd, published 1976

Adele Davide for 'Hare'

James Hepburn for 'White Hare' by Anna Wickham, first published in 1971 by Chatto & Windus in *Selected Poems*

Ian Serraillier for 'Anne and the Fieldmouse', © Ian Serraillier 1982

The Society of Authors for 'The Goat Paths' by James Stephens, © Mrs Iris Wise

Ursula Stuart Laird for 'The Tenant'

James MacGibbon for 'The Hound of Ulster' from *The Collected Poems of Stevie Smith*, published by Allen Lane

John May for 'A Fox Met in a Dream'

Jonathan Cape Ltd for 'Stopping by Woods on a Snowy Evening' by Robert Frost

George Allen & Unwin for 'A Small Dragon' from *Notes to the Hurrying Man* by Brian Pattern

A. P. Watt Ltd for 'Two Songs of a Fool' by W. B. Yeats from *The Collected Poems*, published by Macmillan and reprinted with the permission of Michael B. Yeats and Anne Yeats

Beaver Books for 'Family Holiday' by Raymond Wilson

David Higham Associates for 'My Mother Saw a Dancing Bear' from *Collected Poems* by Charles Causely, published by Macmillan

Stanley Cook for 'The Budgie', 'Growing Grass' and 'Silverfish, Spiders and Flies' from *Come Along*, published by the author

Oberon Press, Canada, for 'The Worm' by Raymond Souster

A. P. Watt Ltd for 'Henry and Mary' by Robert Graves from *The Collected Poems*, published by Cassell

Olwyn Hughes for 'Mushrooms' from *The Colossus* by Sylvia Plath, published by Faber & Faber, © Ted Hughes 1967

Andre Deutsch for 'First Song' from *Poems of Night* by Galway Kinnell, published 1978

Kay Hargreaves for 'Legend'

Alan Jackson for 'Goldfish'

Anna Pollock for 'Happiness' by Erica Marx

Every effort has been made to trace the copyright owners of material used in this anthology. If notified of any omissions the publisher will be glad to make the proper corrections in future editions.

The compiler also wishes to thank her two successive editors, Alison Sage and Caroline Sheldon, whose enthusiasm has made all work a pleasure, and especially Caroline Roberts for her practical and critical help throughout.